MURKY WATERS & CLEAR SKIES

Murky Waters
and Clear Skies

Priyanka Mehta

Murky Waters and Clear Skies by Priyanka Mehta

Copyright © 2020 Priyanka Mehta

This paperback edition published in February 2020
Edition: 1st

Cover photograph © Geetanjali Mehta

CONTENTS

For Life,

dear, dear Life,

sorry and thank you.

There is nothing I love
more than this life that I have,
and yet look how poorly I honor it.

PROMISES

I don't know, I don't know
what will shatter you,
but I know that there is
nothing in this entire world,
that can keep you from
putting yourself back together.

Life is a coming alive,

in the face of certain death.

/

Temples turn to dust, the shrine of

the heart even time cannot efface.

O DE TO A CITY

So warm and beautiful
are your streets,
when I die I will roam
in them unbound,
so lovely are your million
burning lights,
I drown in them each day,
like silence decaying in the
arms of sound.

Bit by bit I lose myself to time,
but still by your promises
each day I am found,
and all that was by fate so
furiously caged,
still by your listless love
is ever so gently unwound.

One day I will fall into

your waiting dust,

and rise like a phoenix,

unafraid, unbound,

and because I lost myself to

your infernal silence,

one day by the everlasting

symphony of paradise,

I know I will be found.

Stay humble, castles built on pride are the first to fall, while the hut of the humble, survives the ages.

Honor the memory of those who are gone,

by living the life they never could.

/

Don't run too hard, the world is round,

and life always goes in circles.

What is the worth of one life?

It is priceless, for you cannot honor

the many, without first honoring the some.

Power reveals the monster in men,
the monster that slumbers under fear of
insignificance and anonymity.

/

Our lives are so filled with
longings, it is impossible to tell
where they end and we begin.

ROADS

Keep walking,

through all the good and the bad, the right days and the wrong ones. There is no stopping along the way, there is no giving up, not even for a moment, because if you stop, you will start sinking into the sand and once you've known despair for too long, you will want to know nothing else.

Just keep moving, one day at a time, one moment at a time; keep walking into the future until the very last day of your life. Keep going, until you turn up on that day and then you can stop. Stop and look back and smile at your journey one last time, before letting it go and walking on into something new and beautiful.

How many wars have been fought,

how many lives have we lost,

for the ambitions of a few.

/

Sometimes we do what is right,

for all the wrong reasons.

I hope that who you are, always matters more to you, than what you have and what you do.

All your life, people will perceive you differently,
treat them all the same.

/

Everything knows its purpose
here on Earth, everyone except us.

The heart of a child is always light and free, not because it has everything it needs, but because it needs nothing to be happy.

Time always tells the truth,

Time itself is a lie.

/

I am filled with pride by the things
I did wrong, but dared to do anyway.

—

ODE TO A REFLECTION

I am faithless

on some days,

on some days

I am hopeless,

but I am relentless

every single day,

and every day still,

I am breaking less

and becoming more,

singing to the ocean

but walking on the shore,

every day I am growing back

the wings that I tore,

and I am far from doubtless,

but closer, closer to being sure.

There is no fooling fate,

it knows no kings nor paupers,

only pawns.

/

The fragrance of flowers will

disappear, the memory of

kindness will stay forever.

—

When the mist of ignorance clears, you will realize, you were never really lost in the first place.

Tell the tale of a thousand tears,
with a smile on your face, a smile that
no storm can ever wipe away.

/

The sum of all our dreams,
is the life that we live.

We are players in a game of cosmic proportions, there is no use fighting something so enormous and divine.

It is always better to go against the tide,

than against the grain.

/

The lights around you might blur,

but the spark within, the spark

within no night can never dim.

BEAUTIFUL

My every day is not beautiful,
it is fractured and obscure and
at times just a little bit strange.
My every day is not beautiful,
but when I look back
and the days all become one,
a life rises from out of the chaos;
a life that is meaningful,
a life that is purposeful.
All the fractured bits fit into
each other perfectly and from
the madness rises design, a design
that reveals, even if for a moment,
its maker's benevolence.
My every day is not beautiful, but life is…
beautiful and if you look closely enough,
just a little bit spectacular.

The weight of the world vanishes,
when on the wings of hope,
my dreams they take flight.

/

When we go looking, no matter what
the question, what we are always,
always seeking, is ourself.

The heart knows no death, it simply becomes love and rises like a rainbow, when the body it vanishes.

Broken birds can sing still,

and their songs can make

even stones fly.

/

Who said you are incomplete, creation

it is always perfect, perhaps it

are our eyes that are dusty.

—

We are broken people, when we are trying to be someone else. The harder we try, the more we break, but every now and then when we stop, just like that, we become whole and beautiful once again.

Bridges rise when the dream,

becomes bigger than the dreamer.

/

Breaking the sky before dawn, will

not make the sun come out any sooner.

ODE TO A DREAM

If I could,
I would fill your life with a thousand roses,
but I know that they come with their thorns,

and I would build castles for you,
castles that can last a thousand dawns,
but I know that caged birds can never sing,
and there is no freedom in being bound,
bound by golden strings.

And so I do what I am most afraid to,
I close my eyes and set you free,
hoping someday your smiles will
find their way back to me,

and light up my slumbering world,
so that once before my time is done,
I know what it feels like,
what it feels like to stand in the sun.

—

Sunrise to sunset, dusk to dawn,
keep your eyes on the road and walk on.

/

Save the songs of your heart,
for those who need nothing
more than your silence.

—

Little by little, paradise is perfected right here on Earth, by hands that refuse to be defined by their circumstances.

Our songs are silent, but strong
enough to make the universe,
sway to their symphony.

/

My arrows are all dipped in honey,
I dare not break what I did not create.

Every tree is a lesson. If a little seed buried in the mud can, in time, grow into such a magnificent being, imagine what we can become, with just a little bit of patience.

Hold onto things long enough,

and you will let yourself go.

/

The direction of my day is decided,

by what I wake up believing in.

—

CLOCKS

Time is not the true measure of one's life. Like a flower's fragrance remains long after it has been plucked, and like the stars whose light fills our sky ages after they are gone, so does the love we give and the courage we sow, remain buried in time.

And like a seed in the desert, touched by the first rain, a simple act of kindness blossoms into joy in a stranger's heart in some distant future.

Time is not the true measure of a life, but love is; the love with which we live, the love that we give others, and the love that we show ourselves.

It is not who I am today that you
should fear, but who I can be.

/

If everything is lost,
you will be found.

—

Nature is always at peace with itself. Look how many miracles it accomplishes, simply by accepting life's design with humility.

Save something for the seasons to come,

too much today can drown the desert,

long before spring can touch its door.

/

Dangerous are those who think

they know everything.

Instead of walking the same road that millions before you have done, find a new way, forge a new path, so that when you are gone, your footprints can lead others who come after you, to places they thought were impossible to reach.

In time, our biggest mistakes
become our greatest teachers.

/

No one remembers yesterday more
than the one who wasted it.

—

ODE TO A WARRIOR

If no one is doing what is right,
let it be you,

if one by one they close their eyes,
and no one can see the truth,
let it be you,

if they pretend to listen,
but fail to give life its due,
let it be you,

if they fall into darkness,
and refuse to see a way through,
let it be you.

Let it be you who sees the light,
let it be you who holds
the torch in the night,
let it be you who tells

—

the wrong from the right,

let it be you who can see

the black and the white,

and when there is nothing

more left to do,

and to the inevitable they

refuse to surrender to,

let it be you, let it be you.

Fight the world if you need to, fight life if you want to, fight people if you have to, just don't fight yourself. That is one war you will lose, even if you win.

Life lingers at the edge of uncertainty each day, only some know how to dance to its boundless possibilities.

/

Nothing deserves our mercy, more than us.

Don't let the words of strangers shatter you, don't let the silence of familiar faces hold you back. There is no joy in seeking vengeance, there is no peace to be gained, in honoring others before yourself.

Life is a love for all things
insignificant and absurd.

/

But we are mortal here child,
why pretend to lord over
what we are prisoners of.

—

ODE TO THE LOST

Wherever the road takes you,

whether life makes or breaks you,

whether love claims or forsakes you,

I will always look at you and smile,

whether it takes a moment or a while,

I will walk the longest mile,

so that I can be there at the end

when you return,

and when the tides they do turn,

we will light a fire together, light a fire

and watch the worlds burn.

Life can be lived,

or lived through.

/

Nothing will define you as much as defeat, and
what you chose to do with it.

—

There is no safety in following your heart, it leads you where you are most afraid to go. But if you don't follow it, you will never really know, what was waiting for you, beyond the edge of the night.

All things are magnificent,

all things a little mundane.

/

Pass on all the good that you receive, let the bitter

drown with you in the merciful oceans of time.

LETTING GO

Sacrifice. It is the one thing no one ever talks about. The sacrifices that they had to make, all the dreams and the hearts that had to break on the way to something beautiful. The thousand tears that had to flow, all the smiles that had to go, all the happiness they could never know, because they were on their way. On their way to something great, something extraordinary, something bigger than themselves. Sacrifice is the bridge across the limitless ocean; it is the boat with which you cross the raging rivers of life. Sacrifice is the fire that burns you to pieces, and from those ashes it forges you a kingdom, a kingdom that you have never known before.

Some things are necessary,

nothing is vital.

/

It is not important what happened,

what is important is what can still happen.

—

Everything has its place,

everything has its season,

only ripe fruits are sweet,

only a full grown oak, useful.

There is nothing more extraordinary,
than finding solace in the ordinary.

/

We take for granted our tomorrow, but
until you realize it is not promised,
you can never truly honor the present.

ODE TO THE STARS

I have diamond in my eyes,

and everywhere I look,

all I see are stars,

some sweet, some shy,

some who like a river rush all day,

some who stand aside and wonder why,

everywhere I look,

I can see the spirit that never dies,

maybe you can blame the wind,

or maybe, maybe you can blame

the diamond in my eyes.

The future is a fallacy,

we spend our lives chasing

what does not exist.

/

Out of seven billion lives, you are one,

and that is all it takes, just one

to change everything, forever.

—

I have battled giants wearing the garb of faith and always won, because there is no one more faithless than them.

Our darkest hours come uncalled,
much like our blessings, for they
come from the same place.

/

There is greatness in winning,
but glory in losing and
losing gracefully.

—

FIREFLIES

There is no grand and final answer.

There is just a succession of little days that we gather like fireflies in a jar, on and on until the vessel is full and then we set them free and call it a life lived.

There is no great and final answer, there is just a learning to live intensely in the little moments, so that in time, the fireflies we gathered day after day after day, rise together like the sun, when our time here is done.

Life has no meaning, until we do something
meaningful, with the time that we have been given.

/

The love that we leave lingers forever, what
is of dust made, disappears.

Sometimes I wonder, how is it that we have been able to reach the stars, but we are still at war with ourselves.

ODE TO THE ANGELS

I've been telling lies all my life,
walking the edge of a knife,
with a smile on my face,
so you won't see, see
my fall from grace.

But time it can efface
the mightiest mountain,
and within me now
rises a fountain,
ready to burst through,
tainting my world blue
with its crimson hue.

And the rain of regrets
falls over me like diamond dew,
leaves me wishing I knew,
what it was like to be free,
of the chains that are stitched
with glue into my skin.

—

64

But running from yourself
is a race you can never win,
and so I let it go and into
the silence I sink,
walking at the brink
of the unknown each day,
on and on until even death
cannot make me stay,
nor stray from the path
I never could choose,
nor could I refuse.

For once destiny was forged
and my fate sealed,
and the truth under vices
of wickedness concealed,
I plunged into the world
of the living and forsake,
remembering myself
until I was awake.

And so all I have now are
whispers so frail,

haunting me

day and night like a gale,

so strong it can sink ships

and raise empires,

for within me rages an inferno,

a volcano that never tires,

and even when I walk through

a thousand fires,

this loyal shadow it

abandons me not.

And when the battles

have all been fought,

still it returns to

remind me once again,

that I may pretend all day

but I pretend in vain,

and no matter how many

bridges I dare to burn,

a kingdom still awaits,

still awaits my

triumphant return.

The sun shines on everyone, some use it to build bridges to new worlds, others to burn their world to ashes.

True friendships last long after
the hearts that held them, have
stopped beating.

/

Look for the beautiful underneath the bizarre,
and you will find the magnificent
hiding beneath the mundane.

—

H O M E

We are a hundred miles
from home,
or perhaps a thousand,
what does it matter,
with every step that I take,
the fragrance of its love
that is etched in my heart,
makes bridges across the
impassable ocean and fills
this strange world with a
familiar scent.
We may be a million
miles from home,
and yet home is here,
throbbing within me still,
like a sacred symphony.

The greatest gift you can ask for,

is to one day see things

for what they are.

/

I am a prisoner of my thoughts,

a slumbering master.

The roads you take, will all lead back to you, go gently then, go gently, for you don't have far to go.

ODE TO AN ISLAND

There is an island,
an island where
no one knows my name,
no one cares who I am
or from where I came.

They laugh all day,
until twilight steals
their wakefulness,
and then fall into
slumber peacefully,
grateful for the watchful
moon's gentle caress.

And when the sun rises,
a smile blossoms on every face,
they may have nothing,
but their hearts are always,
always overrun with grace.

—

Today, tomorrow,

joy and sorrow,

all things and days

are the same to them,

gratefully, gratefully from

nature a little they gather,

as gently, gently through every

weather like giants they walk,

and the wind it dances when they talk,

enchanted by the silent beauty,

of mere mortals living like life,

is but a sacred duty.

One day when you have

conquered your kingdoms

and honored your pride,

I will take you there

across the ocean wide,

and you will see

how a handful of earth

heaven became,

unseen, unknown, on an

island with no name.

Nothing is final here except death.
As long as you are living, anything can happen, as
long as you are living, everything can happen.

/

Gather only what you need,
the journey is long and
the climb steep, too steep.

WHO YOU ARE

Strip away everything,

the name you carry,

the family you were born into,

the who you are and what you do,

all that you have and the things

you seek, take it all away and what

is left is you. The real you.

The you that time cannot efface,

and life, dear life cannot kill.

The you that you've been seeking

in hollow mirrors and empty spaces.

Strip away everything and in one breath,

in one breath you are home.

Life cannot be lived
in bits and pieces,
either you live
completely and fully,
or you don't live at all.

A LIFE

When was the last time, you took a breath, that was not laden with the weight of the world.

When was the last time you smiled without making the edges of your heart bleed with tears of regret.

When was the last time you were unafraid and unbound by the expectations and anticipations of life. You've been you for so long, you've forgotten what it felt like to be free. Free not of the world or its vulgarities, but free of yourself. Free of your thoughts and your emotions, free of the pain and the past you carry in careful packets like it is precious gold. Free of fear that comes in waves every second that you are alive.

It is an overwhelming thing, to be alive, to be aware of so much and yet to understand so little. It is not something they teach you in school, making through days that seem intent on tearing you to pieces. There

—

are no books for it, no words that can even come close to assuaging the storms that rage within, even when the world that you are in, is calm and pristine. All that there is, is you. You are the problem and the solution. The good and the bad, the right and the wrong, the is and the was and the will be, they all matter because you are trying so hard to be you. You have created these roles and parts for yourself, that you then have to spend the rest of your life playing.

You are the winner, the loser, the parent, the child, the lover, the hater, the seeker, the pessimist, the optimist, the dreamer, the believer, the grateful, the hopeless. You are trying to be so many things, you don't even realize when you stop being you.

So who are you really then...maybe this and that and a billion other mirrors. Or maybe you simply are just you. As you were when you came into this world, as you will be moments after you leave, when all the pretence and artifice you accumulated slips away and there is nothing left but you.

You did not come into this world to be somebody, you came here to stop being, because only when you stop being this and that and all those things that you are not, do you become who you've always been. A life that is boundless, a life that is free, a life that is infinite and unfettered in possibilities.

This is what we are made of,

a little faith, a little sadness,

a little sanity, a little madness,

a handful of dust and a grain of

that which never dies, we are

boats then, boats caught between

murky waters and clear skies.

Made in the USA
Middletown, DE
29 July 2022

70193772R00057